THE MASKS WE WEAR

The Masks We Wear

Langston Brown

The Masks We Wear
© 2025 Langston Brown
Cover Art © 2025 Langston Brown
ISBN: 979-8-9987811-6-2

Published by Youth Writer's Press
Colton, California
youthwriterspress.com

First Edition, 2025

To request permissions, you may contact the Publisher at
info@youthwriterscamp.com

Printed in the United States of America.

Cover design by Langston Brown & Emily Anne Evans
Layout design by Emily Anne Evans / Photon Moment LLC

CONTENTS

FOREWORD

Langston,

What a powerful name

Your light has always proven to never dim

You are me and I am you

You made me a Boy mom

You taught me patience and resilience

You loved me when I was broken

Took all my pieces and made me whole again

I love you until infinity

When you are lost

Like a lighthouse

Remember I will always be home

Like the North Star

Follow me

When you feel fatigued

Lost

Remember I will always give you my strength

As you gave me yours without knowing

I love you son and I am so proud of you. You are truly amazing and remind me each day to be grateful even when times are difficult. When you were four years old

and could not speak— as everyone else worried I knew
that you were waiting on your time. This collection of
poems is only a small look into a voice you are still finding
on your own time.

Love,
Mom

The Masks We Wear

CHAPTER 1

the masks we wear for others

Masks of betrayal

We all wear masks even if we think we don't,
we lie to friends at the thought of protecting them,
in the end not knowing we harm ourselves
conclusion using our emotions as an illusion
hiding our feelings under our own emotional mirage
using false feelings as a facade.

Hate of smile

Even if we cry, smile, or stress we hide under a lie
fearing going the extra mile
treating our emotions like a dial
putting ourselves in a trial of hate, stress, and anxiety
of the network in our mind leaving ourselves behind.

CHAPTER 2

emotional actors

Butterfly of lies

Just like an owl butterfly pretending to be its predator
We pretend to be others knowing we won't live up to
their expectation
Filling the void in their hearts but not our own
Leaving us empty inside making us want more, but still
not filling the void in our hearts
Restarting the cycle of torment on our offspring and
students, but we have to break the cycle of emotional
manipulation ourselves
Actors of the emotional spectrum
We are like actors changing personalities for others but
not ourselves
Pushing everybody to the frontlines
Leaving our own selves behind
Making us lose the race of life
Stabbing you in the back; leaving a crack of resilience
Some people see as brilliant
Not knowing the truth of the smile on your face.

Motion of lies

Fake emotions are like a motion that only the truth can
stop until you open up.
You will be locked in a cage of your own feelings,
leaving a scar that's always healing,
but never closing,
but still posing as fine,
until you cross that line.

CHAPTER 3

untold fear

Underneath a smiling face,
Nightmares bloom in a hidden space,
Terrors whisper in its wake,
soft and low
an outwardly feeling I let it not show.

Lurking shadows always near,
darkness held, a silent fear.
A little fear, it hides inside,
a secret place, where worries ride.

It does not shout, it does not cry,
just whispers low, as days go by.
A fear unseen, a fear unspoken,
a fragile trust, easily broken.
It stays so still, behind a smile,
and waits a long, and lonely while.
For someone kind, to see it there,
and help it breathe, in open air.

A little fear, no name,
hides deep, a silent flame.
It doesn't shout or cry,
just waits, inside, close by.
A shadow in the day
that won't quite go away.

CHAPTER 4

fear of expression

A worry, soft and low,
a place you cannot go.
It lives in whispered thought,
a battle never fought.
An untold, unseen dread,
keeps secrets in your head.
A cold knot in the gut, unnamed, unacknowledged,
like a shadow just beyond the light, always there,
breathing.

It doesn't need a reason, doesn't need a name,
just the quiet hum of dread, an echo in the bones.
The untold fear,
a silent roommate.

CHAPTER 5

hidden anger

Garden of hatred

Beneath the smile
a silence grows
a garden choked with thorny rows.
The voice is calm
the hands are still
but rage runs deep
a buried will.
It wears a mask of measured grace
yet flares behind a passive face.
A glance too sharp
a laugh too thin
the war is waged
beneath the skin.

Internal hatred

No shattered glass
no shouted word
just echoes no one ever heard.
A clenched jaw in the dead of night
a dream that ends in a silent fight.
It simmers low
it waits its turn
a lesson anger learns to burn.

Storm of anger

Not in the open
not in flame
but in the places none can name.
So tread with care where shadows lie
where fury learns to pacify.
For even peace can wear a disguise
and hold a storm behind its eyes.

CHAPTER 6

true tears

Seasonal tears

Like the first rain drop of an untamable storm,
a singular tear is a fear that most understand
but that's a future we must band.

Chambers of the heart

In the quiet chambers of the heart where feelings dwell,
where whispers of love and joy in silence swell,
lies a riverbed,
dry and cracked,
longing for a spell
that would release the true tears,
and make it tell.

Desert of despair

A tale of agony – a saga unseen,
where souls are torn apart
where hearts have been.
In the vast desert of despair
hope's a mirage
so thin
yet... the promise of true tears
is where it's kin.

CHAPTER 7

fake smiles

Mask of smiles

Smiles can be like a mask we wear.
We want to take them off,
but fear what would happen to us if we.
But as we age the mask begins to tear,
we begin to lose that fear,
and true emotions can be near.

Emotional lies

Even as we lie, we want to lie with fake emotions.
We want to show our true emotions,
so we must show our true tears or hidden anger.
We have to show our true emotions.

Liars smile

A simple smile could be a lie,
only seen by the naked eye.
A false feeling like artificial water,
but as time goes your feelings begin to falter
and truly show
We fear our emotions as much as we fear death,
but death is a beauty only pure people can see.

CHAPTER 8

lies of smiles

Masquerade of joy

A masquerade upon the face,
a smile that hides the hidden ache,
a fleeting glow, a hollow grace,
a silent plea behind the fake.
In the shadows of a crafted grin
lies stories unspoken, deep within.
Yet beneath the mask, a truth still waits
a fragile heart that yearns for fate.

CHAPTER 9

my mask

Love of the unknown

The fear of the unknown
could be anything a killer
an animal
the monster under your bed
or the monster in your head
but they forget that love is the unknown
I found that out in 1st grade I loved a girl who I walked
with every school day
but I lost my chance to tell her my feelings years ago,
leaving my emotions scrambled
happiness being indeed sadness sadness being
relievement and love being self hatred

Smiles of disguise

Born from mistakes of hopes and dreams
of my mother and father
no trust from a mom who loves me like the earth loves
the moon
and a father who believes in me as much

No title

as we believe

the future will thrive

only having God by my side

and bearing the pain

of losing my loved ones

from the past and present

in my life wearing a smile

as a disguise

Traumas dance

Even as tears rundown my face there's no sadness,
not even a trace but pain.
I can never forget the scar on my right eye,
the sirens ringing in my ears,
the cries of my mother.
Not knowing what to feel
I cry out still in pain,
but that feeling never stopped,
but now I smile.

CHAPTER 10

war masks and battle cries

Oceans mighty emotions

As waves hit the shores
They cry out of struggle to relieve the past
Holding it tight, while emotions grow bigger
Like a storm- tsunami of your feelings
Ship wrecked or marooned on your own isle of
emotions
Nothing holding on to the past besides the fear of
showing your true self in front of your naval fleet
Only you control these waves of emotion pushing your
friends in motion but abandoning yourself behind.

An army of love

A musical soldier
Melodies of angelic songs you are the one who uses
your talent for war and peace.
Your music notes are your bullets ending your enemies
the more you sing only being limited to your vocals,
you carry out your wishes not only singing for our army
America but also.... God,
you connect family, putting them before your own
mental health.

ABOUT THE AUTHOR

Langston is a 13-year-old writer and art enthusiast. He enjoys art in all of its forms and uses every day as a place to play and imagine. This collection of poems is his second published work. Follow Langston on Instagram: @blackboyspaint.

youthwriterspress.com

A program of Youth Writer's Camp, Inc., Youth Writer's Press exists to create a safe space where young voices are heard, valued, and amplified. We are dedicated to producing and publishing work that allows youth to share their truths with the world. Our mission is to equip the next generation of writers with the resources, confidence, and platform to turn their stories into lasting works that resound far beyond the page.

youthwriterscamp.com

This book was created as part of Youth Writer's Camp, Inc., a nonprofit organization whose mission is to motivate communities to redefine hope for young people through mentoring, enrichment, and creativity.

In our workshops and programs, we blend literacy enrichment, social-emotional development, and creative entrepreneurship — using writing as a tool for healing, growth, and community connection.

Youth Writer's Camp Values:

COURAGE Creating the strength to face challenges with confidence.

RESILIENCE Creating the ability to bounce back and keep moving forward.

EMPATHY Creating connections by truly understanding others' feelings.

AUTHENTICITY Creating a space where you can be your true self without masks.

TRANSPARENCY Creating an atmosphere of openness and honesty, where vulnerability is valued.

ENTERPRISING Creating opportunities through innovation and a dynamic mindset.